I Don't Want To Go to Bed

Poems about bedtime
Angela Marie James

Copyright © 2025 by Angela Marie James

All rights reserved. This book or any portion thereof may not be reproduced or used in any manner whatsoever without the express written permission of the publisher, except for the use of brief quotations in a book review or scholarly journal.

First Printing: 2025
ISBN: 979-8-8829-9751-8

Angela Marie James
Staffordshire

www.amjames.co.uk

Cover designed by Getcovers

Dedication

Dedicated to all children who some nights just 'don't want to go to bed' and the parents who tirelessly get them to sleep.

I just love writing poetry; it is so much fun. Why not have a go yourself!

Feel free to add to some of my poems, write your own versions and have fun asking others to guess who or what you are.

Books by Angela Marie James

FOR YOUNGER READERS

I Don't Want To
I Don't Want To Go to Bed
I Don't Want To Eat That (Due out in 2025)
I Don't Want To Go to School (Due out in 2025)

Guess the Animal
Guess the Farm Animal (Due out in 2025)

I Can't Wait
I Can't Wait for Christmas (Due out in 2026)

FOR OLDER READERS

Conflict Poetry
Conflict
Lest We Forget (Due out in 2025)
Damaged Earth (Due out in 2026)

Visit www.amjames.co.uk for more details

You can read some of the poems from the upcoming book
I Don't Want To Eat That
at the end of this book

Contents

1. I Don't Want To Go to Bed - Part 1   1
2. Close, Close, Close My Eyes   3
3. First Night in My Own Room   4
4. My Bedroom   6
5. One More   8
6. My Blanket   9
7. I'm Scared   10
8. I Don't Want To Be in Bed - Part 1   12
9. I'm Not That Ill   14
10. The Magic of Books   15
11. I Don't Want To Fall   16

12.	Time to Go to Bed	18
13.	She Hid It	19
14.	I Don't Want To Go to Bed - Part 2	20
15.	I'm Hurt	21
16.	Squashed	22
17.	Nightwear	23
18.	I Wish My Bed Was	24
19.	Five More Minutes	26
20.	Sleep	27
21.	I Don't Want To Be in Bed - Part 2	28
22.	Why Are You?	29
23.	The Illness	32
24.	Duvet Days	34
25.	Under the Cover	35
26.	Too Tired	36
27.	Bedtime	37

28.	Alarms	38
29.	I Don't Want To Go to Bed - Part 3	40
30.	Sleepovers	41
31.	I Want to Sleep	42
32.	Under the Bed	44
33.	I Hate Tidying My Room	45
34.	I'm Sorry	46
35.	Dreams	48
36.	I Don't Want To Be in Bed - Part 3	50
37.	Ten Sleepy Children	51
38.	Bath Time	54
39.	I Wish I Was a Parent	55
40.	Is it Morning Yet?	56
41.	A Boy Called Ted	58
42.	I'm Not Sleepy	59
43.	My Window	60

44.	The Attic	62
45.	Night	64
46.	I Don't Want To Go to Bed - Part 4	65
47.	Another Night in Bed	66
48.	Story Time	67
49.	I Need to Tell You	68
50.	I Don't Want To Wake Up	70
51.	Answers	72
52.	Resources	73
53.	Preview of I Don't Want To Eat That	74
54.	I Don't Want To Eat That - Part 1	75
55.	Eat, Eat, Eat Your Food	77
56.	The First Time I Ate	78
57.	My Kitchen	80
58.	One More	82
59.	My Lolly	83

60.	I Don't Want To Books	85
61.	About Angela Marie James	87
62.	How to Find Out More	89

I Don't Want To Go to Bed - Part 1

I don't want to go to bed
I'm not tired
I'm still hungry
I need another drink

I'm scared
I feel really sick
I've missed you
I need to tell you something

Do I have to go to bed?

No, they're not excuses
I really can't get to sleep
It has nothing to do with
Wanting to stay up late

So I can carry on playing
Finish this game
Read more of this book
Spend more time with you

Do I have to go to bed?

What, you mean if I stay awake
I'll still have to get up early
No matter how tired I am
I won't be able to nap during the day

I'll also need to go to bed early tomorrow
But that's so boring
I'd rather stay up then instead
Do you know what?

I think I'll try to go to sleep!

<u>Close, Close, Close My Eyes</u>

(To the tune of Row, Row, Row Your Boat)

Close, close, close my eyes
Try to get to sleep
Wishing, wishing, wishing, wishing
I could play instead

First Night in My Own Room

My first night in my own room
I'm both scared and excited
It's great to have my own space
But I'll miss my little sister

We had so much fun sharing
A bedroom together
But our new house is bigger
So we have a bedroom each

I have so much more space
To spread out all of my toys
They won't get mixed up now
Or broken by little hands

Maybe we won't fight as much
Or get on each other's nerves
But I'll miss our late night chats
When they think we're fast asleep

It's scary being on my own
But I'm a big girl now
I don't even need a nightlight
To help me get to sleep

I am excited as well
As I get to decorate
My room the way I want
Which will be lots of fun

It may seem strange for a while
But I'll soon get used to it
My room is going to be great
Deep down, I just know it

My Bedroom

My bedroom is
A school of magic
Where spells are cast galore

My bedroom is
A farm
Full of animals to care for

My bedroom is
A castle
Which I defend from intruders

My bedroom is
An alien planet
With lots of areas to explore

My bedroom is
A story land
Where favourite characters come to life

My bedroom can
Be lots of things
Pretending is so much fun

Your bedroom can
Be lots of things too
Just use your imagination and play

What else do you think your bedroom could be?

Have fun thinking of different things!

Have a go at adding to my poem by writing your own idea in the same style as I have.

Grab a piece of paper and have fun!

One More

One more story
One more drink
One more hug
One more kiss

One more game
One more snack
One more talk
Before bedtime

My Blanket

Warmth-giver
Tear-wiper
Den-builder
Costume-maker
Seat-coverer
Soft-hugger
Child-hider
Comfort-provider

I'm Scared

I'm scared

Of the monsters under my bed
Hiding in my wardrobe
Crouching under my desk

I'm scared

Of the strange noises at night
Hearing creaking and banging
Listening for intruders

I'm scared

Of the shadows when it's dark
Weird shapes on my wall
Wondering if they'll move

I'm scared

Of the tapping on the window
Wondering what's outside
Hoping they can't get in

I'm scared

Of falling asleep at night
In case I have bad dreams
Making me shake and shiver

I'm scared

Of lots of things at bedtime
Keeping me wide awake
Even though they're not real

I Don't Want To Be in Bed - Part 1

I don't want to be in bed
It's messy all the time

You scrunch me up tight
In your little hands
Over and over

Scrunching, scrunching, scrunching

Which might not sound too bad
But then it gets worse

You twist me around you
When you're fast asleep
Over and over

Twisting, twisting, twisting

But that is not all
There is much more

You kick me about
As you toss and turn
Over and over

Kicking, kicking, kicking

Even in the daytime
There is no escape

You even mess me up
When you play on me
Over and over

Messy, messy, messy

I never stay clean
Or neat for very long

You only tidy me
When your parents say
Over and over

Tidy, tidy, tidy

Who or what am I?
Turn to the back of the book for the answer!

I'm Not That Ill

I may be ill
Way too ill for school
But I'm not that ill
To stay in bed all day

The Magic of Books

My books are like magic

Hidden behind the covers
Is a place of wonder
Taking me somewhere new
Every time I pick one up

I get to go on adventures
Explore the unknown
Meet lots of people
Find out things I didn't know

My books are like magic

I get to be someone else
When I read a book
Live their life for a while
Shut everything else out

I could read all the time
If I got the chance
I often keep on reading
Instead of going to sleep

I Don't Want To Fall

Oh please, please be careful
I don't want to fall
I'm scared of where I'll land
If I'm knocked off the bed

Now listen here you pesky child
Just look what you've done
I'm falling, falling down below
Then knocked under the bed I go

It's dusty and dirty down here
What am I to do?
And now I'm getting all creased
Oh pray, please pick me up

Now I'm getting ignored
Oh, when is this torture to end?
You watch, you'll forget about me
That will drive me round the bend

I'm on my own all day long
In the dark under the bed
Wondering if when you come home
You'll notice that I am gone

Oh wait, a hand approaches
Am I to be kidnapped now as well?
Clutched out from the darkness
Suddenly blinded by the light

I'm pulled out very carefully
Placed down flat and pressed
Page by page to straighten me
Making me look more like my best

Then I'm picked up and carried
Lovingly in someone's arms
Along with others lost like me
To be put back in their homes

Not a bad end to a rough day
Warm and safe and sound
Ending up pride of place
Back on your bookcase once more

Who or what am I?
Turn to the back of the book for the answer!

Time to Go to Bed

Time to go to bed
Pack away, pyjamas on
Wash and brush your teeth

She Hid It

My sister just hid it
I don't know why
She just came up to me
Grabbed and hid
My favourite teddy bear

I was upset and so I cried
Which made her laugh
So, I opened up my
Mouth and screamed!
As loudly as I could

My Dad came upstairs to me
He asked what was wrong
So, I pointed at my sister
Glared and shouted
"She hid my teddy bear!"

My sister was told off and
Told to give me back my teddy
But before she did
She smirked and said
"You'd better look after your things!"

I Don't Want To Go to Bed - Part 2

I start off all nice and warm
When you dress in me for bed
But it's not long until it's
Time to put clothes on instead

Then I'm shoved under the pillow
Get left on the floor
Am kicked under the bed
Or caught under the door

Sometimes I'm forgotten
Discarded and unclean
Until your parents ask for me
To go in the washing machine

Then I am washed and cleaned
All nice until you next wear me
When once again I'm discarded
In the morning when you leave

Who or what am I?
Turn to the back of the book for the answer!

I'm Hurt

I've hurt myself once more

Cut my hand
Bruised my foot
Trapped my finger
Banged my head

Tripped over a box
Got hit with a toy
Scraped my knee
Fell down on the floor

Medicine cupboard, here I come

Antiseptic wipes
Cold compress
Sticky plasters
White bandages

Lots of attention
Kisses where it hurts
Reassuring hugs
Please let me stay up

<u>Squashed</u>

Squashed, squashed
Is how we feel
When picked up by you

Teddies, cats
You squash us all
When taking us to bed

One night
We had a dream
That we were very big

This time
We had come
To squash you tight instead

<u>Nightwear</u>

Soft smooth snuggly nightwear
Cosy cuddly comfy onesies
Sequined sparkly swirly nighties
Cool cute character pyjamas
Fluffy fuzzy funny slippers
Soft smooth snuggly nightwear

I Wish My Bed Was

I wish my bed was

A tree house
Then it would be
A great place to hide

I wish my bed was

A racing car
Then it would be
Fun to drive

I wish my bed was

A plane
Then it would be
Amazing to fly

I wish my bed was

A time machine
Then it would be
A great way to explore

What else do you think your bed could be?

Have fun thinking of different things!

Have a go at adding to my poem by writing your own idea in the same style as I have.

Grab a piece of paper and have fun!

Five More Minutes

Five more minutes
I just want to finish this game
Then I promise I'll get to bed

Five more minutes
I just want to finish this book
Then I promise I'll get to bed

Five more minutes
I just want to finish this film
Then I promise I'll get to bed

<u>Sleep</u>

Sleep can be an adventure
Lost in magical dreams
Endless places to explore
Each time is something new
Plenty to see and do

I Don't Want To Be in Bed - Part 2

I don't want to be in bed
I get knocked and bruised
I'm never left alone
When it's bedtime

I don't want to be in bed
Everyone climbs on me
Bounces on me
Stretches out on me

I don't want to be in bed
I just get so tired
Of everyone lying on me
Not caring for me at all

Who or what am I?
Turn to the back of the book for the answer!

Why Are You?

Parent:
Why are you still awake?
You know you should be asleep
Is there something wrong?
You know you can tell me

Child:
Err, no, not really
There is nothing wrong
I'll try to go to sleep
From now on

Parent:
Why are you jumping?
Making all this noise
You've woken up your sister
She can't get back to sleep

Child:
Err, I'm just so excited
To go to my friend's tomorrow
I'll stop jumping
From now on

Parent:
Why are you playing?
It's bedtime, not playtime
You're making a right mess
On your bedroom floor

Child:
Err, I'm just so bored
I couldn't get to sleep
I'll put it away and play
In the morning

Parent:
Why are you talking?
You know you should be quiet
Is it something you'd like
To share with me?

Child:
Err, no, not really
I'd really rather not
I'll try to be quiet
From now on

Parent:
Why are you crying?
Are you hurt?
Or are you thinking of
Those bad dreams again?

Child:
Err, no I'm not hurt
I'm just scared to go to sleep
In case the dreams come back
Please stay with me?

The Illness

I felt as gloomy as a dark rain cloud
The day I started to feel ill
I worried about it all day long
Scared I'd be sent to bed to rest

I shook like a jelly on a plate
As I didn't like feeling like this
I tried really hard to ignore it
To concentrate on something else

I must have looked as white as a sheet
When Mum came in with the medicine
I tried really hard not to be sick
As I swallowed each spoonful down

I grinned like a circus clown
When I started to feel better
I'd coped with staying in bed when ill
Now I could move about again

I felt all warm like a hot water bottle
Recalling how I'd been cared for
I found I'd enjoyed the attention
Now I won't be so worried next time

Duvet Days

I love duvet days
Snuggling up together
Watching lots of films
Spending time together
Family time is great

Under the Cover

Instead of going to sleep
Under the bed cover, I go
So that I can read or play a game
Hiding so no-one will know

Too Tired

Too tired to play
Too tired to draw
Too tired to read

But never tired enough to sleep

Too tired to bake
Too tired to eat
Too tired to drink

But never tired enough to sleep

Too tired to tidy
Too tired to clean
Too tired to help

But never tired enough to sleep

Too tired to wash
Too tired to brush
Too tired to dress

But never tired enough to sleep

Bedtime

Bedtime
Is so boring
It's the worst time of all
I just want to play all night long
No sleep

<u>Alarms</u>

Alarms
We wish we didn't have to use

Alarms
Are what parents tell us to set

Alarms
Interrupt our wonderful dreams

Alarms
We try very hard to ignore

Alarms
Can be so very, very loud

Alarms
Annoy us until we get up

Alarms
We shout at a lot

Alarms
Try to wake us at the right time

Alarms
We turn off to go back to sleep

Alarms
Should never have been invented

Alarms
Are what we forget to turn on

I Don't Want To Go to Bed - Part 3

I don't want to go to bed
The other teddy is mean to me
He teases me, calls me names
Pushes me out of the bed

He just won't leave me alone
I don't know what to do
I normally like going to bed
But he makes me not want to go

<u>Sleepovers</u>

I love
Sleepovers
I so look forward to them
Talking, laughing, playing, eating treats
Staying up watching films
I just can't wait
Can you?

I Want to Sleep

I get so bored
Sleeping in my bed
I want to try
Somewhere else instead

I want to sleep

Inside my wardrobe
In the empty bath
Crammed in my toy box
Curled up on the mat

I want to sleep

Under the table
Behind the sofa
Inside a cupboard
Beneath the window

I want to sleep

Next to the flowers
In the long grass
Under an oak tree
Spread out on the path

This might be fun
But in the end
I think I would miss
My warm and comfy bed

Under the Bed

I went under my bed to look for something
But instead, I came out with the following
One storybook
Two Lego bricks
Three odd socks
Four pyjama tops
Five used tissues
Six broken pencils
But I never found what I was looking for
I guess my dressing gown is lost forever more

I Hate Tidying My Room

I hate tidying my room
I like it the way it is
It may seem messy to you
But I know where everything is

I'm Sorry

I'm sorry

I've really tried
To get to sleep
My head really hurts
Get the medicine, please?

I'm sorry

I've really tried
To get to sleep
I'm very thirsty
Glass of water, please?

I'm sorry

I've really tried
To get to sleep
But I'm not tired
Tell me a story, please?

I'm sorry

I've really tried
To get to sleep
I'm just so worried
Can you help me, please?

I'm sorry

I've really tried
To get to sleep
I hear strange noises
Look over there, please?

I'm sorry

I've really tried
To get to sleep
I'm just really scared
Will you stay longer, please?

What else do you think could be stopping you from getting to sleep?

Have fun thinking of different things!

Have a go at adding to my poem by writing your own idea in the same style as I have.

Grab a piece of paper and have fun!

Dreams

I often dream
When I go to sleep
I wonder which type
Of dream I'll have tonight

Will it be a good dream?
Will it be exciting?
Will it be a bad dream?
Will it feel frightening?

Will it be a new dream?
Will it be strange?
Will it be an old dream?
Will it not change?

Will it be a silly dream?
Will it be surreal?
Will it be a sad dream?
Will it seem very real?

I often dream
When I go to sleep
I hope I'll remember
The dream when I awake

I Don't Want To Be in Bed - Part 3

I don't want to be in bed
I get squashed every night
Head tossing and turning
Hands pulling and grabbing
No-one cares if they hurt me
When their head lies on me at all

Who or what am I?
Turn to the back of the book for the answer!

Ten Sleepy Children

Ten sleepy children
Sitting in a line
One helped their dad
And then there were nine

Nine sleepy children
Staying up late
One went to bed
And then there were eight

Eight sleepy children
Talking of heaven
One felt sad
And then there were seven

Seven sleepy children
Showing each other tricks
One got bored
And then there were six

Six sleepy children
Pretending to fly
One hurt themselves
And then there were five

Five sleepy children
Stretched out on the floor
One got cramp
And then there were four

Four sleepy children
Watching TV
One got scared
And then there were three

Three sleepy children
Not sure what to do
One left the room
And then there were two

Two sleepy children
Trying not to yawn
One fell asleep
And then there was one

One sleepy child
Sitting on her own
She cuddled up to Mum
And then there were none

Bath Time

I hate bath time
It is never any fun
No splashing or playing
Instead, it's just boring washing
I wish I didn't have to have a bath

I Wish I Was a Parent

I wish I was a parent
I wish I was in charge
I'd tell everyone what to do
It would be a blast

I'd never set a bedtime
I'd never tell children off
Devices could stay on
With us all night long

No more baths or showers
No more brushing teeth
We'd just play every night
Instead of going to sleep

Is it Morning Yet?

I can't wait until morning
It's my birthday tomorrow
Cards, presents, parties, cake
I love them all, don't you?

All excited
I cannot wait
So, I ask once again
Is it morning yet?

I can't wait until morning
We go on holiday tomorrow
Pools, beaches, arcades, fairs
I love them all, don't you?

All excited
I cannot wait
So, I ask once again
Is it morning yet?

I can't wait until morning
It's Christmas Day tomorrow
Santa, stockings, presents, turkey
I love them all, don't you?

All excited
I cannot wait
So, I ask once again
Is it morning yet?

A Boy Called Ted

There was a young boy called Ted
Who hated going to bed
He would shout and scream
Say he'd had a bad dream
So he could go in mum and dad's bed

I'm Not Sleepy

I'm not sleepy
I'm wide awake

I'm not yawning
I'm not dozing
My head is not dropping
Nor am I snoring

I'm not sleepy
I'm wide awake

My Window

When I can't get to sleep
I stare outside my window
Gazing up at the stars
Searching for constellations

Sometimes I see movement
Up in the sky above
A shooting star, a UFO
But usually just a plane

I listen out for cars
But there are not that many
Out at this time of night
Most people are at home

Sometimes I see movement
On the darkened streets below
As dog walkers pass by
Pulled by their faithful friend

I look across the street
At the other windows
Wondering what's going on
Behind the dark curtains

When I can't get to sleep
I stare outside my window
Thinking how many others
Are wide awake like me

The Attic

What's in the attic?
Why aren't we allowed to go up?

Is there a magical wardrobe?
Which can take us to faraway lands

Are there lots of presents?
Which they don't want us to find

Is there a treasure chest?
Which holds precious things

Are there lots of old toys?
Which we're not allowed to play with

Is there a mystical portal?
Which can take us back in time

Is there lots of chocolate?
Which they secretly eat at night

What's in the attic?
Why aren't we allowed to go up?

What else do you think could be in the attic?

Have fun thinking of different things!

Have a go at adding to my poem by writing your own idea in the same style as I have.

Grab a piece of paper and have fun!

Night

Night
Cold, quiet
Sleeping, dreaming, resting
Bedtime, darkness, light, morning
Talking, laughing, playing
Noisy, warm
Day

I Don't Want To Go to Bed - Part 4

I don't want to go to bed
I enjoy being out at night
Lighting up the sky
When the sun goes down

Who or what am I?
Turn to the back of the book for the answer!

Another Night in Bed

Another night in bed
Boring as can be
Children sleeping all night long
Dreaming endlessly
Every night a battle
Forcing myself to sleep
Groaning when it's time to get up
Happy when allowed to lie in

Story Time

It's story time
My favourite time of day
I'm as happy as can be
I wonder where we'll go today

I Need to Tell You

Before I go to sleep
I need to tell you
What happened today
It just can't wait

Before I go to sleep
I need to tell you
About my best friend
It just can't wait

Before I go to sleep
I need to tell you
How unwell I feel
It just can't wait

Before I go to sleep
I need to tell you
What my brother did
It just can't wait

Before I go to sleep
I need to tell you
About my new game
It just can't wait

Before I go to sleep
I need to tell you
How worried I am
It just can't wait

Before I go to sleep
I need to tell you
About my bad dream
It just can't wait

I Don't Want To Wake Up

I don't want to wake up
I'm just too tired
I didn't get much sleep
Stayed up way too late

Let me stay in bed

I don't want to wake up
It's way too early
It's still dark outside
Can't be morning yet

Let me stay in bed

I don't want to wake up
I'm way too ill
I feel so dizzy
My head really hurts

Let me stay in bed

I don't want to wake up
It's way too cold
I'm lovely and warm
Wrapped up nice and tight

Let me stay in bed

I don't want to wake up
I'm just too comfy
I don't want to move
My bed is so soft

Let me stay in bed

I hope you enjoyed reading this book as much as I enjoyed writing it.

For the answers to some of the poems, information about free resources and a sneak preview of my upcoming book,
I Don't Want To Eat That*,*
keep reading.

Answers

I Don't Want To Be in Bed – Part 1
Bedding (duvet, blanket, etc)

I Don't Want To Fall
A book

I Don't Want To Go to Bed – Part 2
Pyjamas

I Don't Want To Be in Bed – Part 2
A mattress

I Don't Want To Be in Bed – Part 3
A pillow

I Don't Want To Go to Bed – Part 4
The moon

Have a go at writing your own riddles.

Choose someone or something that either doesn't want to go to bed or doesn't want to be in bed. Think of ways to describe them/it and write it down as a riddle. Then ask someone else if they can guess who or what you are!

Resources

On my website, there is a free activity pack that I have created for this book. It includes art activities, creative writing activities, quizzes and word searches.

This can be downloaded and used by children, parents, teachers, librarians, etc.

You can find it via the following link:

www.amjames.co.uk/i-dont-want-to-resources

Coming Soon

I Don't Want To Eat That

POEMS ABOUT EATING

ANGELA MARIE JAMES

I Don't Want To Eat That - Part 1

I don't want to eat that
It's too hot
I'm not hungry
I've eaten lots already

I don't like it
It tastes horrid
It looks disgusting
What if it makes me ill?

Do I have to eat it?

No, they're not excuses
I really can't eat it
It has nothing to do with
Wanting to eat dessert

So, I can eat ice cream
With sprinkles and sauce
Then rush back upstairs
To carry on with my game

Do I have to eat it?

What, you mean if I don't
You'll save it for me
So, I can eat it tomorrow
Instead of a new meal

I also can't have dessert
But that's not fair
I'd rather eat it now
Do you know what?

I think I'll try to eat a bit more!

Eat, Eat, Eat Your Food

(To the tune of Row, Row, Row Your Boat)

Eat, eat, eat your food
Try to clear your plate
Hoping, hoping, hoping, hoping
You will eat your veg

The First Time I Ate

The first time I ate ice cream
I gobbled it down so quick
That I got brain freeze

The first time I ate a sprout
It made me feel quite sick
I couldn't swallow it

The first time I ate jelly
It wibbled and wobbled
Then fell off my spoon

The first time I ate an orange
It was so very sour
I made a funny face

The first time I ate chocolate
It was so delicious
I wanted lots more

The first time I ate onion
It was so disgusting
I spat it right out

The first time I ate a sweet
I found it so yummy
That I finished the bag

My Kitchen

My kitchen
Is a room of wonder
Where amazing meals are made

My kitchen
Is a treasure trove
Full of lots of yummy treats

My kitchen
Is full of equipment
So, we have to take great care

My kitchen
Is a room of laughter
When we help to bake cakes

My kitchen
Is full of memories
Of lots of fun times we've had

My kitchen is
Lots of things
The heart of our home

What else do you think a kitchen is?

Have fun thinking of different things!

Have a go at adding to my poem by writing your own idea in the same style as I have.

Grab a piece of paper and have fun!

One More

One more chocolate
One more sweet
One more biscuit
One more cake

One more ice cream
One more drink
No more, please
My tummy hurts

My Lolly

Distraction-provider
Tantrum-stopper
Grin-raiser
Stickiness-maker
Sugar-giver
Yummy-taster
Sweet-rewarder

I hope you enjoyed that sneak preview of my upcoming book,
I Don't Want To Eat That

I Don't Want To Books

Coming Soon

About Angela Marie James

Angela has always loved to read and could always be found with her head in a book as a child. Back then, she longed to become an author herself.

So, as an adult, to be writing books for both children and adults is a dream come true.

She loves performing her work and delivering workshops in schools (primary and secondary), nurseries, colleges, libraries, museums, care homes, clubs (e.g. brownies, scouts, holiday/after-school clubs, etc.) and at community events. As well as delivering talks about her work and career.

Angela also enjoys performing and delivering virtual/online workshops all around the world.

If you would like Angela to come to your school, club, etc. (in person or virtually) then please share this book with an adult/teacher.

Details of her author visits and workshops are available on her website (www.amjames.co.uk).

Angela lives in Newcastle-under-Lyme, Staffordshire with her husband and fellow author and illustrator, Glenn Martin James, their two daughters and their two cats.

How to Find Out More

For the latest news about Angela's new books, performances, and other news
Sign up to her mailing list
(via her website at **www.amjames.co.uk**)

Connect with Angela online:
Website: www.amjames.co.uk
Facebook, X, Instagram, Threads & YouTube:
@amjamesauthor

Printed in Great Britain
by Amazon